Wild Weather

Tornado

REVISED AND UPDATED

Catherine Chambers

Heinemann Library
Chicago, Illinois

© 2002, 2007 Heinemann Library
a division of Reed Elsevier Inc.
Chicago, Illinois

Customer Service 888-454-2279

Visit our website at www.heinemannraintree.com

Designed by Steve Mead and Q2A Creative
Maps by Paul Bale
Printed in China by South China Printing Company

11 10 09 08
10 9 8 7 6 5 4

New edition ISBN: 978-1-403-49581-5 (hardcover)
                     978-1-403-49590-7 (paperback)

The Library of Congress has cataloged the first edition as follows:
Chambers, Catherine, 1954-
 Tornado / Catherine Chambers.
            p. cm. -- (Wild weather)
Summary: Describes how tornadoes are formed, the conditions that exist in tornadoes, the harmful and beneficial effects of these storms, and their impact on humans, plants, and animals.
Includes bibliographical references and index.
  ISBN 1-58810-652-7 (HC), 1-4034-0116-0 (Pbk)
 1. Tornadoes--Juvenile literature. 2. Tornadoes – Physiological effect--
Juvenile literature. [1. Tornadoes] I. Title. II. Series.
  QC955.2 .C478 2002
  551.55'3--dc21

                              2002000823

Acknowledgments

The author and publishers are grateful to the following for permission to reproduce copyright material: AP Photo/The Advocate Messenger/Clay Jackson, p28, Associated Press pp 14, 20, 23, 27, China Photos/Getty Images p8, Corbis pp21, 25, FLPA p22, Oxford Scientific Films pp4, 11, 15, PA Photos p26, Photodisc p16, Jim Reed/Corbis p19, Rex Features p12, Robert Harding Picture Library p5, Michael Rolands/istockphoto p29, Science Photo Library pp10, 13, 18, Stone pp7, 9, 17, 24.

Cover photograph of a tornado in Kansas, reproduced with permission of Erik Nguyen/Jim Reed Photography/Corbis.

The publishers would like to thank Mark Rogers and the Met Office for their assistance with the preparation of this book.

Every effort has been made to contact copyright holders of any material reproduced in this book. Any omissions will be rectified in subsequent printings if notice is given to the publisher.

The paper used to print this book comes from sustainable sources.

Some words are shown in bold, **like this**. You can find out what they mean by looking in the glossary.

Contents

What Is a Tornado?

A tornado is a moving, spinning **funnel** of wind. It swirls from a dark, towering cloud. The wind in a tornado is very strong. The tornado can suck up anything in its path.

■ *Tornadoes are formed in dark storm clouds.*

■ *Tornadoes can cause a lot of damage.*

The spinning wind throws everything out at the sides as it moves along. This makes a huge cloud of dust and **debris** around the tornado.

Where Do Tornadoes Happen?

Tornadoes can happen in most places. This map shows some parts of the world where tornadoes happen. There are many tornadoes in the United States.

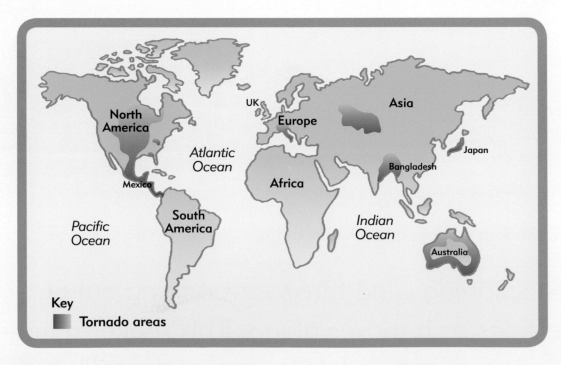

North America
UK
Europe
Asia
Atlantic Ocean
Japan
Bangladesh
Mexico
Africa
Pacific Ocean
South America
Indian Ocean
Australia

Key
Tornado areas

■ *The areas shown in orange are the places where tornadoes often happen.*

■ *This farm is in Tornado Alley in the United States.*

Tornado Alley is the name given to a large area across the middle of the United States. It has more tornadoes than anywhere else in the world.

Wind and Cloud

Wind is made when **masses** of air move around. Some masses are cold. Others are warm. Warm air usually rises. Cold air rushes in to fill the space it leaves. This causes strong winds.

■ *In strong winds, umbrellas can be turned inside out!*

■ *This picture of clouds was taken from space.*

When air rises it cools. The **water vapor** in the air turns into droplets of water and forms clouds. Tornadoes come from some of these clouds.

Why Do Tornadoes Happen?

Tornadoes form in storm clouds. They happen in hot, moist weather. Heavy storm clouds form. Clouds suck up warm, moist air from below. Cool air blows across the top of the cloud. These movements make a twisting wind.

■ *Storm clouds often form in warm weather.*

■ *A waterspout is a tornado over water.*

The spinning wind makes a cone-shaped **funnel** that can reach all the way down to the ground. Sometimes tornadoes move over water. This makes a **waterspout**.

What Are Tornadoes Like?

People can see most tornadoes coming. They can also see dust and **debris** swirling around the bottom of the **funnel**.

■ *Even if you see a tornado it is hard to tell exactly where it will go.*

■ *Clouds that form tornadoes can also make lightning.*

Tornadoes often happen as part of thunderstorms. People see lightning and hear thunder. There is heavy rain and strong winds.

Harmful Tornadoes

The winds in tornadoes travel faster than any other winds. Tornadoes usually only affect a narrow area. They destroy anything in their path.

■ *Some houses can be destroyed by tornadoes while houses next to them are untouched.*

■ *Hailstones can add to the damage caused by tornadoes.*

Some dark tornado clouds hold icy **hailstones**.
When hailstones fall they can hurt people and
animals. They can also damage buildings
and **crops**.

Tornado Alley

The state of Oklahoma is part of Tornado Alley. A lot of damaging tornadoes happen here because the land is so flat.

North America

Pacific Ocean

•Oklahoma City

Atlantic Ocean

■ *Winds can sweep across the flat **plains** around Oklahoma.*

■ *Tornadoes like this one can destroy buildings.*

Terrible tornadoes hit Oklahoma on May 3, 1999. They destroyed everything in their paths. The flying **debris** hit people and buildings—45 people were killed.

Preparing for a Tornado

Weather forecasters keep a careful eye on the weather. When tornadoes are likely to happen, they send out a "tornado watch." If a tornado has been seen, they send out a "tornado warning."

■ *Weather forecasters use computers to help them work out where a tornado will travel next.*

■ *It is exciting to chase tornadoes. It can also be dangerous.*

Storm chasers are people who try to get close to tornadoes. The storm chasers take pictures of the tornadoes. Sometimes they see a tornado first and warn weather forecasters.

Tornado Warning

On April 3, 1974 **weather forecasters** in the United States knew that many tornadoes were coming. They sent out over 160 tornado warnings to 14 states.

■ *Weather warnings can help give people time to prepare for a tornado.*

■ *The 1974 tornadoes were some of the worst in history.*

On that day, 148 tornadoes struck in 13 states. More than 300 people were killed and over 30,000 buildings were destroyed. No one could stop the tornadoes.

Coping with Tornadoes

Tornadoes can damage all types of buildings. In some places, people are able to go to specially built **shelters** when they know a tornado is coming.

■ *Tornado shelters are often underground.*

■ *These cars have been thrown around by a tornado.*

People should not stay in their cars when a tornado strikes. Tornado winds can pick up cars and throw them high into the air.

Tornadoes and Nature

There are many stories of frogs falling from the sky during storms. This is because they can get sucked up by tornadoes. They fall to the ground again when the tornado is over.

■ *Tornadoes over water may pick up frogs or fish.*

■ *Tornadoes can flatten crops.*

Tornadoes often blow across fields where **crops** are grown. They destroy the crops that lie in their path. The paths of some tornadoes are wider than the length of a football field.

To the Rescue!

After a tornado, rescuers often find people trapped in cars or in flattened buildings. Ambulances take **injured** people to the hospital.

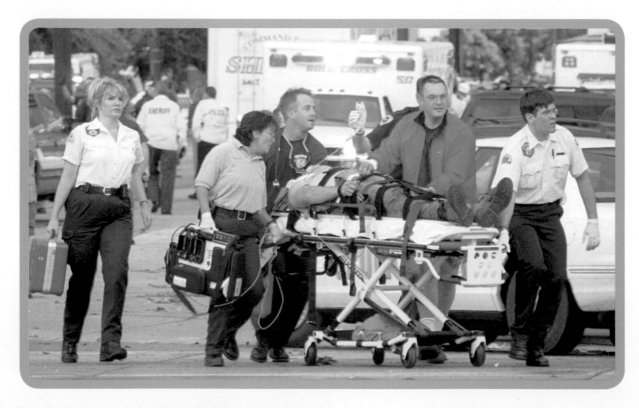

■ *People can be injured by tornadoes.*

■ *It can be dangerous to stay in your home in a tornado.*

Emergency tornado **shelters** can protect people from tornadoes. The tornado's winds cannot destroy them. Their homes may still be destroyed.

Adapting to Tornadoes

People who live where tornadoes happen learn how to take **shelter**. Here, some children are having a tornado drill at school.

■ *People who live in tornado areas must be prepared.*

■ *A siren tells people to prepare for a tornado.*

Areas that have a lot of tornados often have sirens. The sirens make a loud noise when tornados are nearby. People go to the basement, a tornado shelter, or a strong building.

Fact File

◆ The worst tornado that we know about happened in Bangladesh on April 2, 1977. Around 900 people died.

◆ At least 1,000 tornadoes hit the United States every year. More than half happen in the spring, and about a quarter in the summer. More tornadoes happen in April than in any other month.

◆ Scientists use invisible **radio signals** to find out if a tornado is forming. The signals bounce off **ice crystals** in the dark clouds. The signals make a pattern on a computer screen. If the pattern makes a hook shape, a tornado is forming.

Glossary

crop plant grown for food

debris soil and broken objects that are thrown around by the tornado

funnel long, thin tube

hailstone hard ball of ice that comes from some thunderclouds

ice crystal tiny pieces of frozen water

injured hurt

radio signal wave of sound that travels through the air

shelter safe place

waterspout huge funnel of water made when a funnel cloud forms over a lake, wide river, or the ocean

water vapor water that has changed into a gas

weather forecaster scientist who works out what the weather will be like in the future

More Books to Read

Mayer, Cassie. *Weather Watchers: Wind*. Chicago: Heinemann Library, 2006

Royston, Angela. *The Weather: Wind*. Mankato, Minn.: Chrysalis Children's Books, 2004

Index